101
SHOWER
THOUGHTS

Funny thoughts and deep ideas guaranteed to make you smile and say "Why didn't I think of that?"

Squeaky Clean Publishing

www.SqueakyCleanPublishing.com

Introduction

If you bought this book for yourself, or got it as a gift, you probably already know what a shower thought is. But just in case you don't, let me tell you what I think a shower thought is.

A shower thought is an idea or realization that pops into your head at times when you have nothing better to do than think. Like when you're relaxing in the shower for instance. These thoughts can be a better way to do something, or a really good analogy to explain something, or a philosophical idea that blows your mind. When you share your shower thought with someone, the response will be something like "Whoa! Why didn't I think of that?"

In the following pages I've collected my 101 favorite shower thoughts to share with you. I hope they inspire you, make you think, and make you laugh.

At the end of the print edition of the book I've included lined pages for you to write down your own shower thoughts whenever they pop into your own head.

- Larry Neil

Beanbag chairs are
the boneless chickens
of furniture.

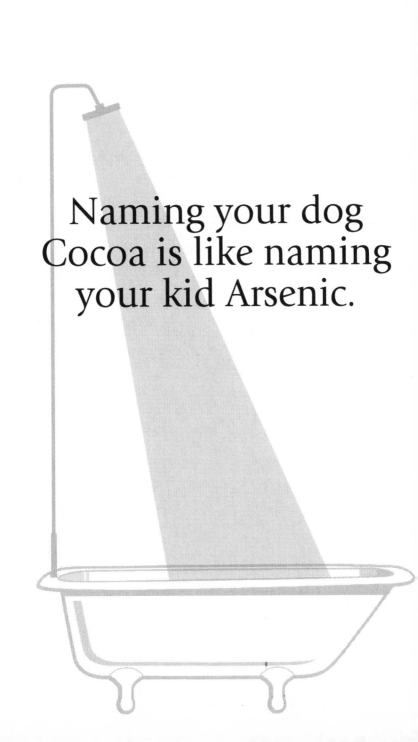

Naming your dog
Cocoa is like naming
your kid Arsenic.

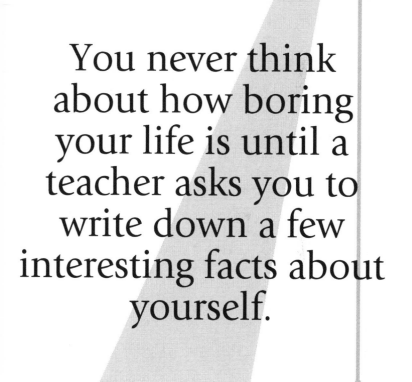

You never think about how boring your life is until a teacher asks you to write down a few interesting facts about yourself.

Anime characters would be much better fighters if they didn't always shout out their next move.

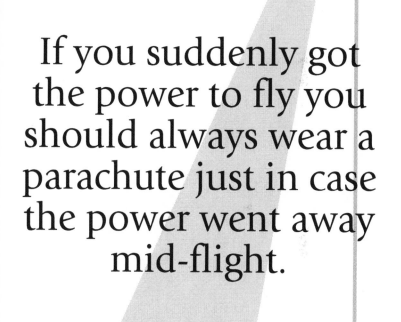

If you suddenly got the power to fly you should always wear a parachute just in case the power went away mid-flight.

An umbrella is a
hand-held portable
ceiling.

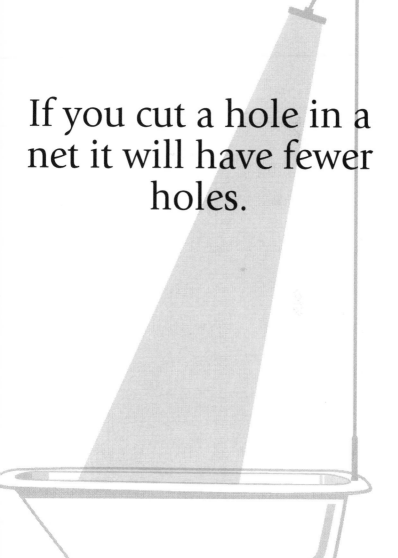

If you cut a hole in a net it will have fewer holes.

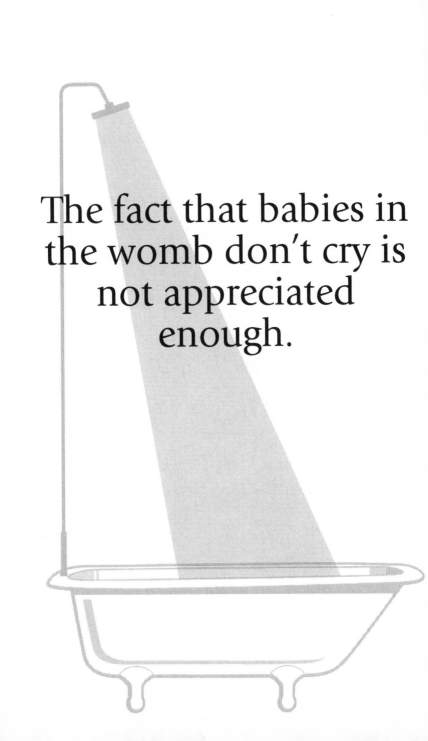

The fact that babies in the womb don't cry is not appreciated enough.

In the wizarding world, rappers would be the hardest to duel. Just imagine how fast they could cast multiple spells.

A child's laugh is a wonderful thing to hear, except when it's in a horror movie.

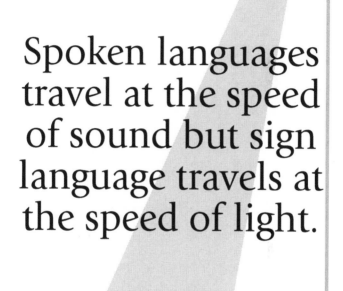

Spoken languages travel at the speed of sound but sign language travels at the speed of light.

Bumper stickers are
tramp stamps for cars.

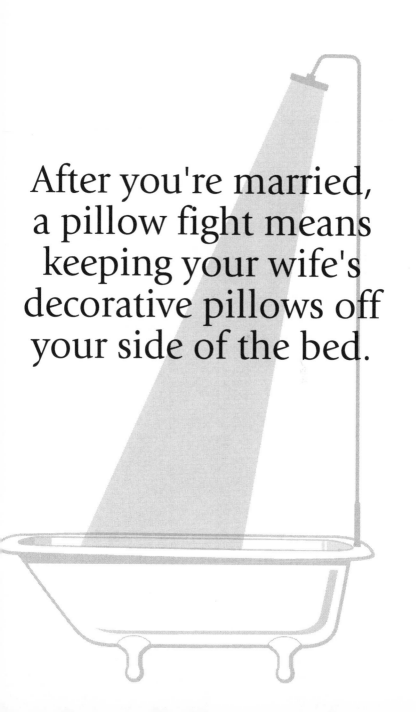

After you're married,
a pillow fight means
keeping your wife's
decorative pillows off
your side of the bed.

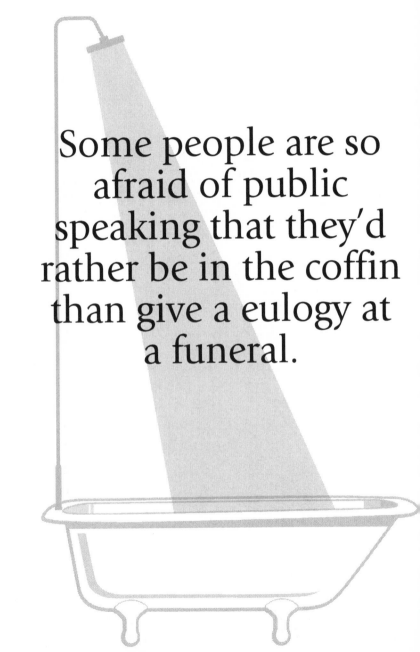

Some people are so afraid of public speaking that they'd rather be in the coffin than give a eulogy at a funeral.

We are all just brains
wearing human suits.

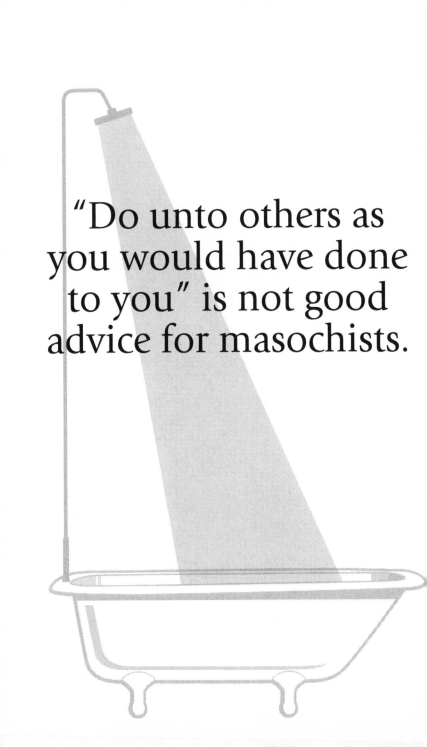

"Do unto others as you would have done to you" is not good advice for masochists.

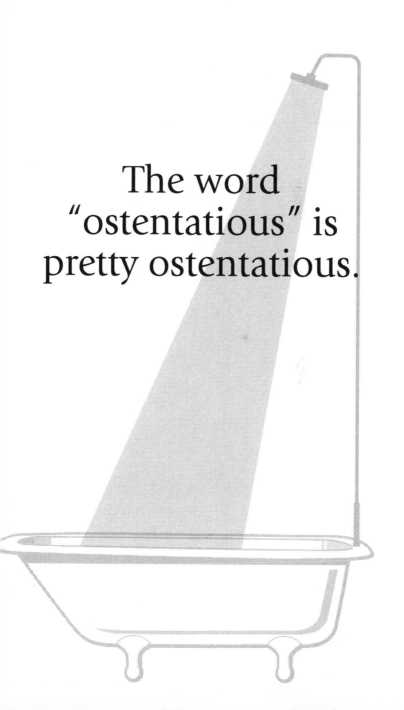

The word "ostentatious" is pretty ostentatious.

The letter "q" is obviously an introvert. You see it very infrequently and when you do it's never without it's friend "u".

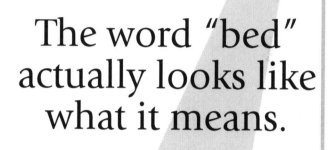

The word "bed"
actually looks like
what it means.

Boneless wings are a marketing ploy that allows adults to order chicken nuggets without feeling silly.

People who work at the unemployment office only have jobs because lots of other people don't.

Your house always seems pretty clean until people are coming over.

Moonlight is solar powered.

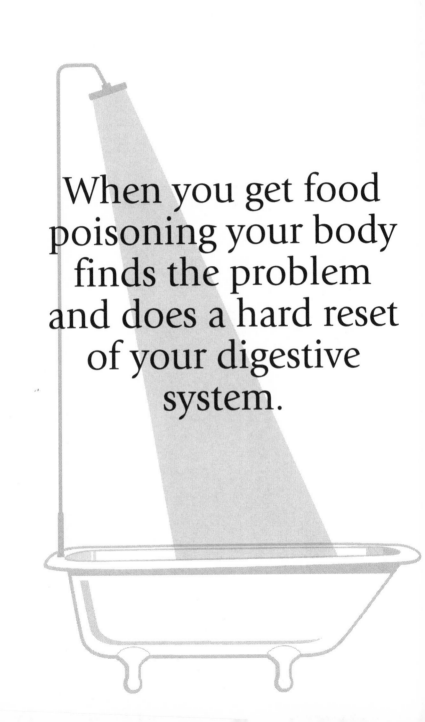

When you get food poisoning your body finds the problem and does a hard reset of your digestive system.

The more napkins you have, the more napkins you'll use.

If there are infinite alternate universes there's probably one where your lame high school garage band made it big.

A thought that keeps you up at night is like a program that's still running that makes your computer unable to shut down.

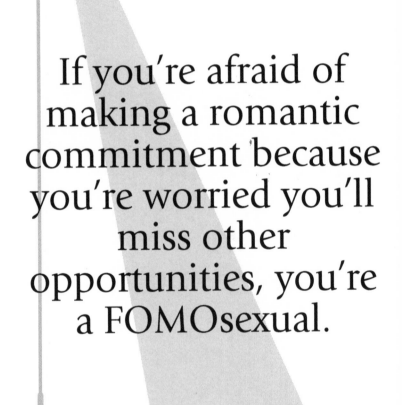

If you're afraid of making a romantic commitment because you're worried you'll miss other opportunities, you're a FOMOsexual.

Children learn to speak in order to complain about their parents more effectively.

Fingernails are small window displays for virgin skin.

Hearing "Pavlov" and thinking of dogs is the most ironic example of Pavlovian conditioning.

Flammable and inflammable mean the same thing.

There has never been a show with the word "Celebrity" in the title that has had celebrities who deserved to be celebrated.

Throwing a ball up in the air is playing catch with gravity.

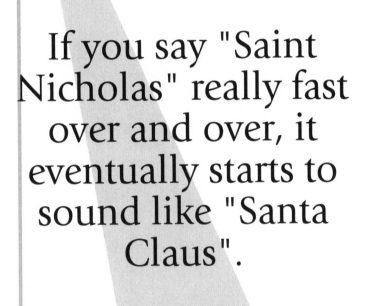

If you say "Saint Nicholas" really fast over and over, it eventually starts to sound like "Santa Claus".

The most useless job
in the auto industry is
installing turn signals
on BMWs.

It would be pretty ironic if we found out that measles cause autism.

Bottled water companies don't actually make water, the make plastic bottles.

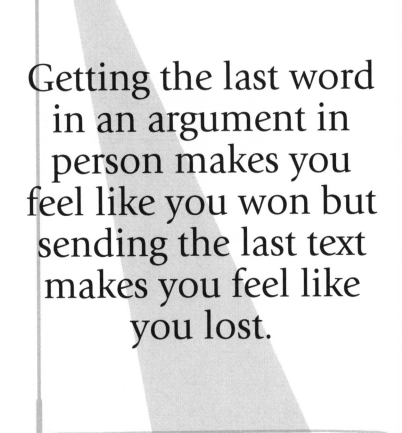

Getting the last word in an argument in person makes you feel like you won but sending the last text makes you feel like you lost.

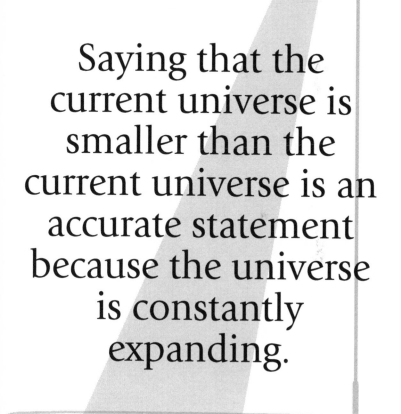

Saying that the current universe is smaller than the current universe is an accurate statement because the universe is constantly expanding.

It's ironic that guns are considered firearms but flamethrowers are not.

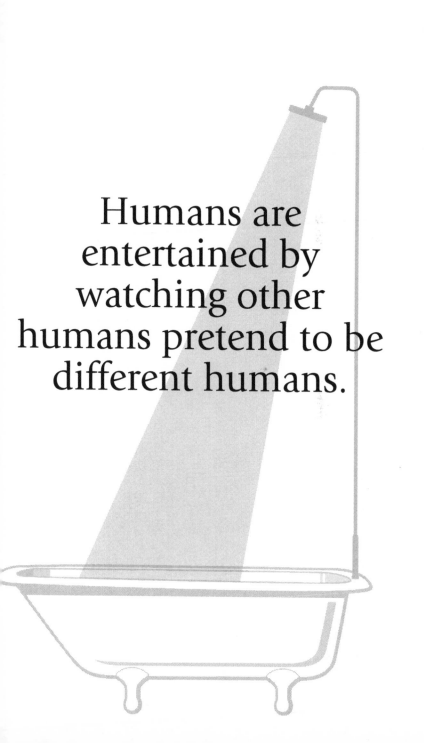

Humans are entertained by watching other humans pretend to be different humans.

Whenever there's an earthquake every Etch A Sketch in the affected area gets erased.

Since most people are buried in suits and dresses, the zombie apocalypse will be the world's largest formal event.

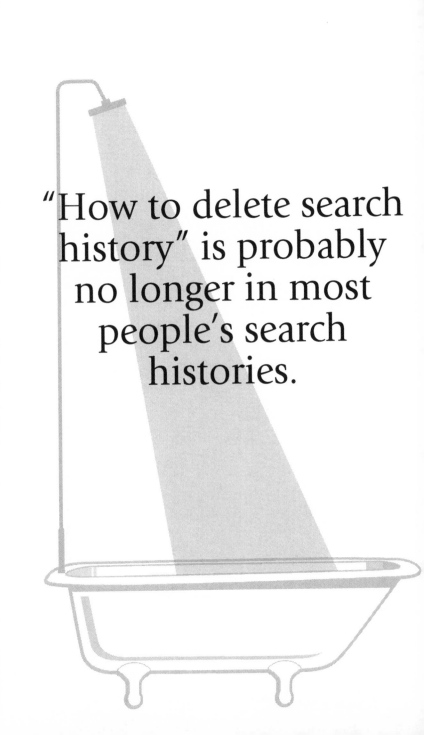

"How to delete search history" is probably no longer in most people's search histories.

You are the most
recent person to
read this.

Fire extinguishers are antiflamethrowers.

If a ghost is a disembodied soul then a zombie is a disemsouled body.

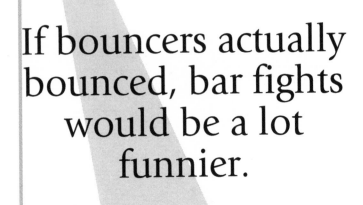

If bouncers actually bounced, bar fights would be a lot funnier.

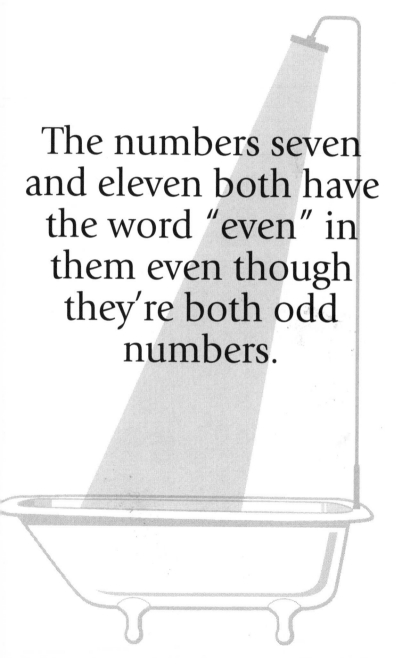

The numbers seven and eleven both have the word "even" in them even though they're both odd numbers.

The ability to talk about nothing is what differentiates friends from acquaintances.

At some point the tv show "Shark Tank" had to be pitched to a room full of investors.

In the past they tried to make home theaters look like movie theaters and now they're trying to make movie theaters look like home theaters.

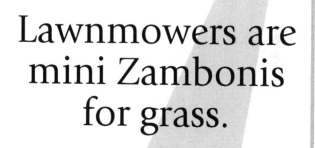

Lawnmowers are
mini Zambonis
for grass.

You never realize how many songs are about dysfunctional relationships until you're in one.

The words "short"
and "small" are
longer than the words
"tall" and "big".

If characters in movies watched more movies they wouldn't make so many stupid decisions.

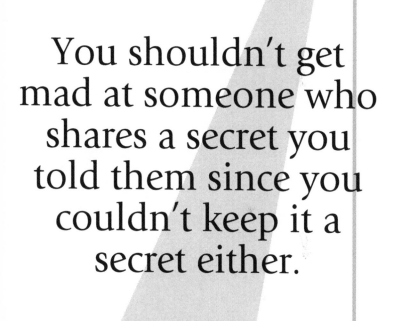

You shouldn't get mad at someone who shares a secret you told them since you couldn't keep it a secret either.

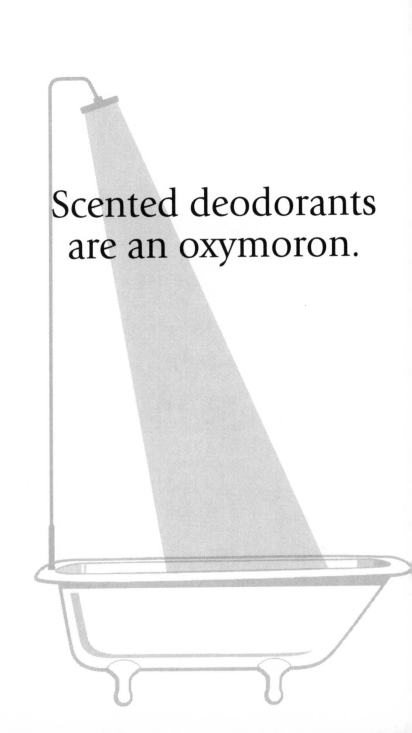

Scented deodorants
are an oxymoron.

3D printers are just
high tech glue guns.

If you see a movie based on a book you love, you'll hate the movie. If you read the book of a movie you love, you'll love them both.

No one actually likes
Choose Your Own
Adventure books.

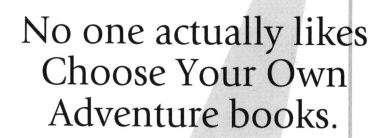

Attractive people with awful personalities are the human equivalent of clickbait.

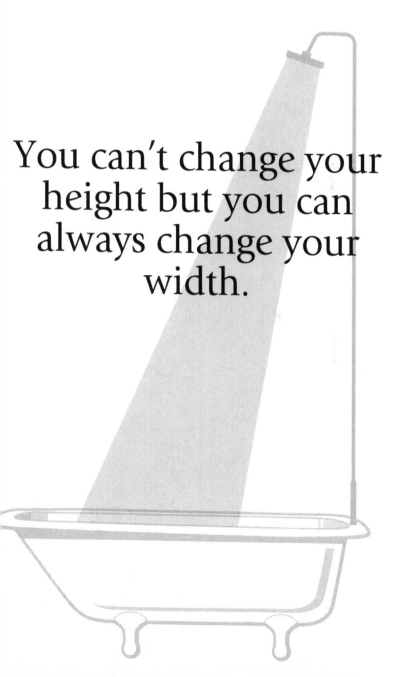

You can't change your height but you can always change your width.

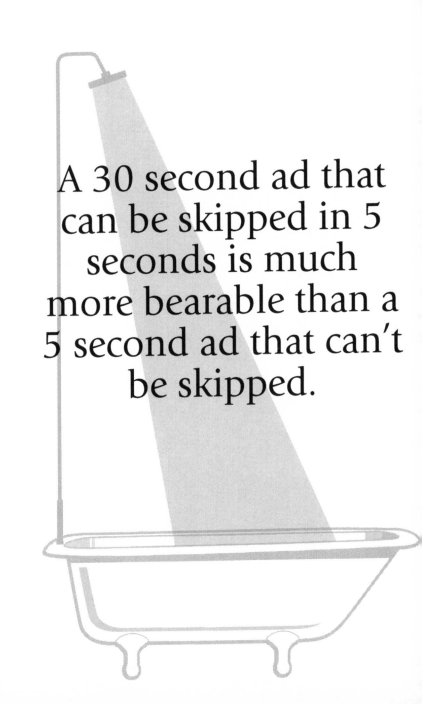

A 30 second ad that can be skipped in 5 seconds is much more bearable than a 5 second ad that can't be skipped.

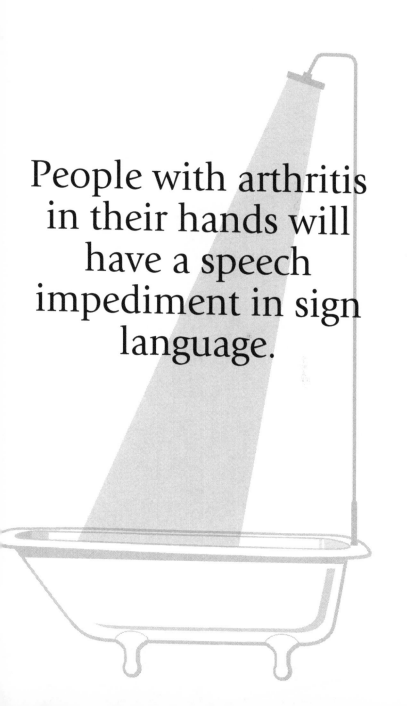

People with arthritis in their hands will have a speech impediment in sign language.

Elevator makers should add the ability to deselect a floor so when you hit the wrong button you aren't forced to go to that floor and stand there like an idiot waiting for the door to close.

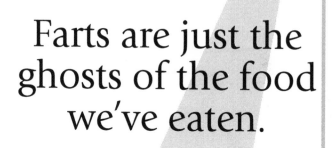

Farts are just the ghosts of the food we've eaten.

In the time since our Grandparents were young, 20 years old has changed from "Why aren't you married yet?" to "You're way too young to get married".

The manbun is the
mullet of Millennials.

Needless to say, the phrase "needless to say" is needless to say.

If you won't wear light colored clothes because they show dirt too easily you're basically saying you don't mind wearing dirty clothes as long as you can't see the dirt.

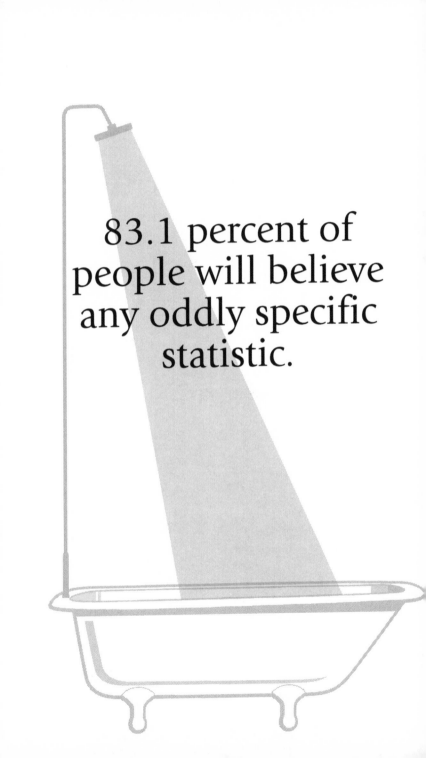

83.1 percent of people will believe any oddly specific statistic.

If you've ever tried to forget something and were successful you wouldn't know it.

The Guinness Book of World Records probably holds the world record for the most world records recorded.

If anti-vaxxers didn't get vaccines when they were kids there would be a lot fewer anti-vaxxers today.

Cat-calling doesn't work any better on women than it does on cats.

Children are like small, broke, best friends, who think you're loaded.

The person who started the tradition of the groom not seeing the bride in her wedding dress before the wedding saved fiancés everywhere from hours of dress shopping and is a hero to all men.

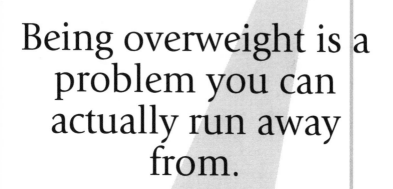

Being overweight is a problem you can actually run away from.

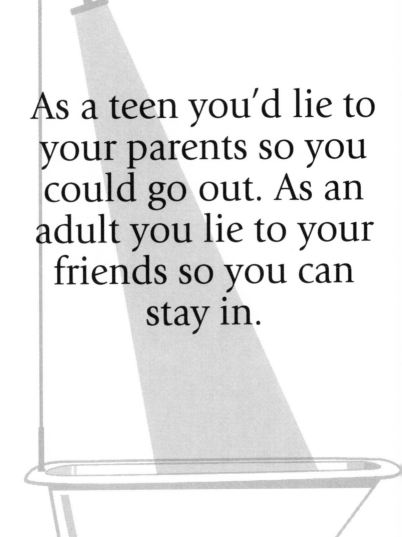

As a teen you'd lie to your parents so you could go out. As an adult you lie to your friends so you can stay in.

A grilled cheese
sandwich is the
American version of
a quesadilla.

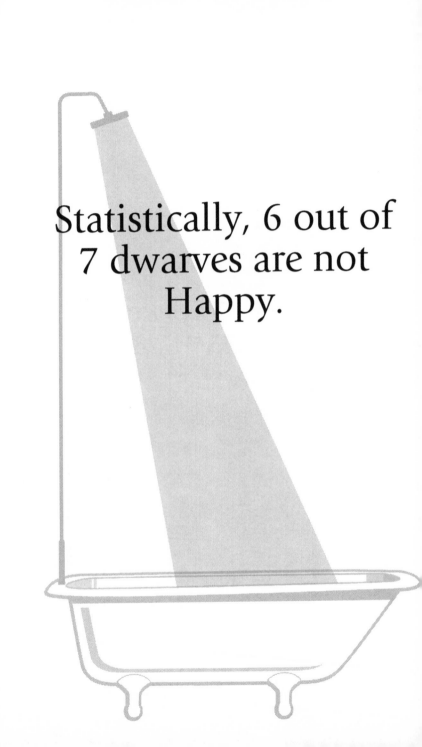

Statistically, 6 out of 7 dwarves are not Happy.

Traditions are nothing more than peer pressure from dead people.

If you ask someone what LGBTQ stands for you'll never get a straight answer.

If love makes you blind, marriage gives you back your eyesight.

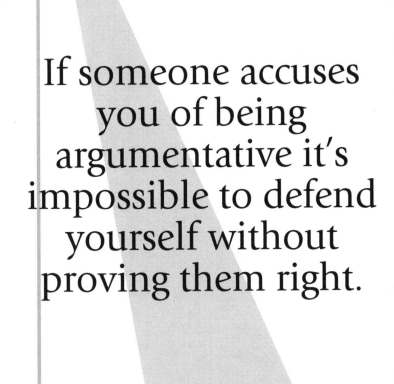

If someone accuses you of being argumentative it's impossible to defend yourself without proving them right.

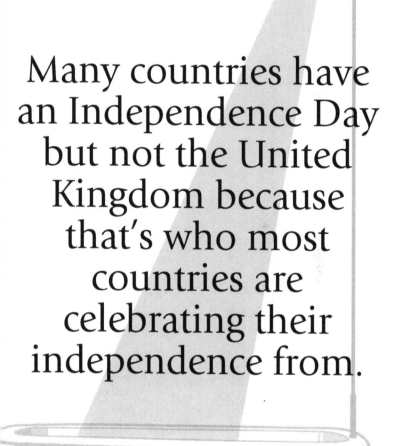

Many countries have an Independence Day but not the United Kingdom because that's who most countries are celebrating their independence from.

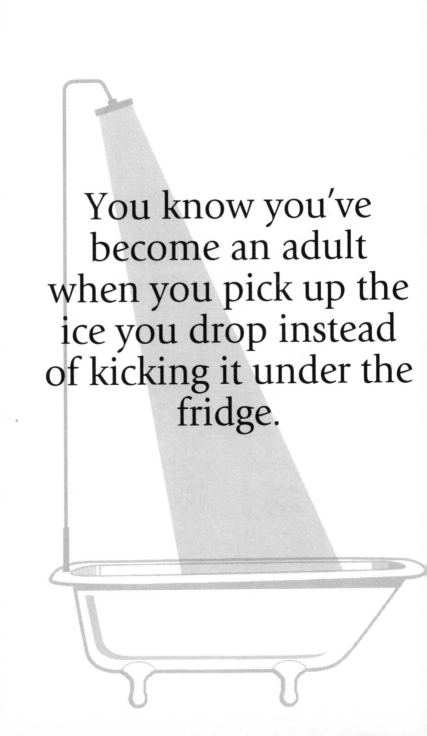

You know you've become an adult when you pick up the ice you drop instead of kicking it under the fridge.

The most unrealistic thing about Harry Potter is that none of his friends at school asked to try on his glasses.

It's ironic that computers freeze when they overheat.

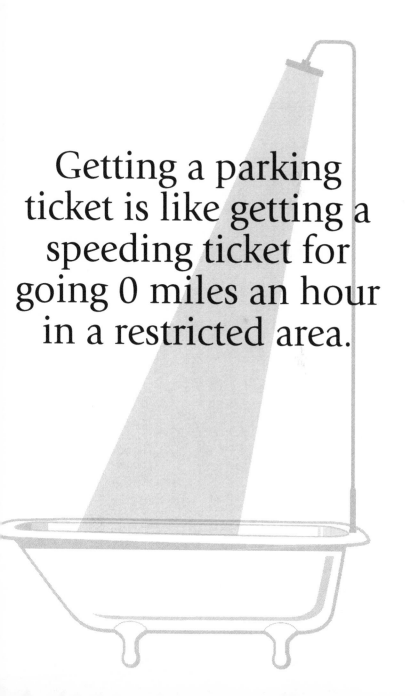

Getting a parking ticket is like getting a speeding ticket for going 0 miles an hour in a restricted area.

For some reason all emotions seem more intense when the person is staring out a window.

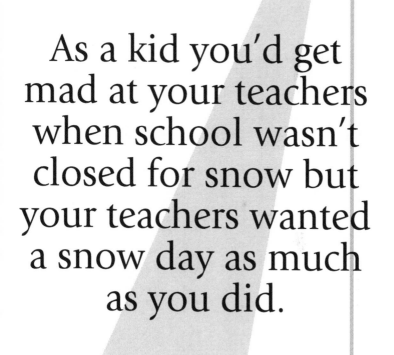

As a kid you'd get mad at your teachers when school wasn't closed for snow but your teachers wanted a snow day as much as you did.

The universe has a weird sense of humor, it seems like every time you lose a sock you gain an orphaned Tupperware lid.

If you have a large stack of resumes to review, take half the resumes in your stack and discard them. This saves you time and makes sure you don't hire anyone with bad luck.

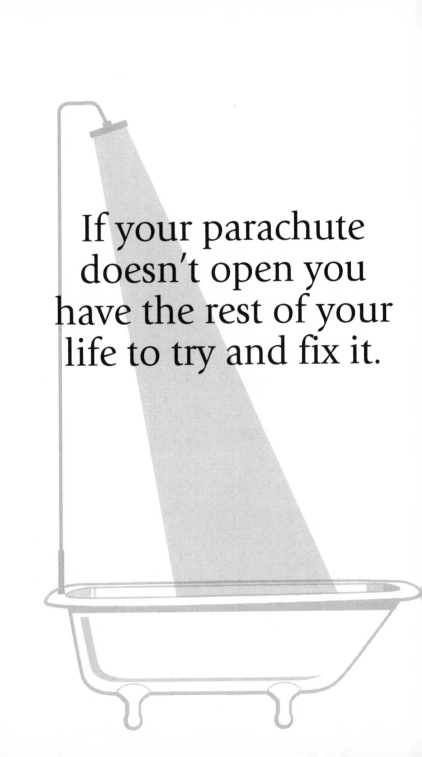

If your parachute doesn't open you have the rest of your life to try and fix it.

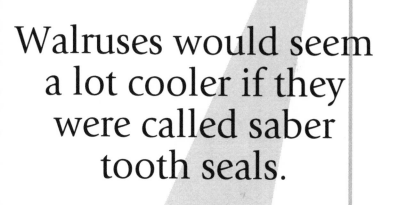

Walruses would seem
a lot cooler if they
were called saber
tooth seals.

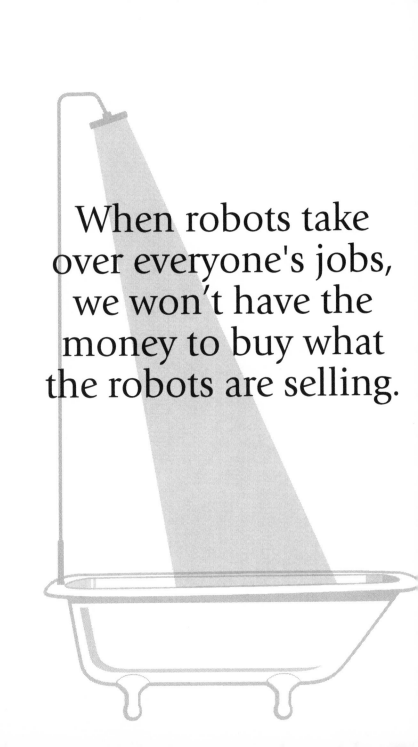

When robots take over everyone's jobs, we won't have the money to buy what the robots are selling.

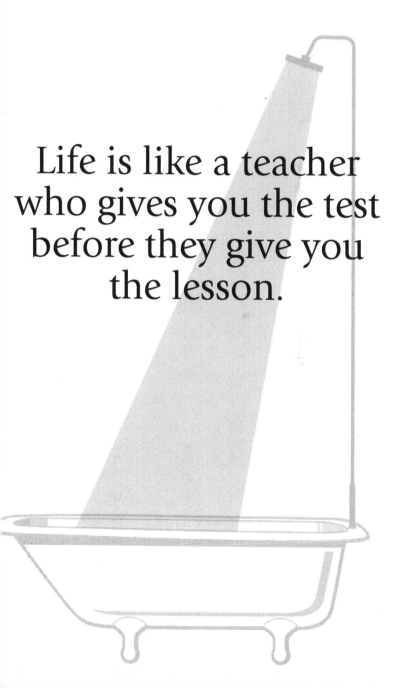

Life is like a teacher who gives you the test before they give you the lesson.

My shower thoughts:

My shower thoughts:

My shower thoughts:

My shower thoughts:

My shower thoughts:

My shower thoughts:

My shower thoughts:

My shower thoughts:

My shower thoughts:

My shower thoughts:

My shower thoughts: